The Finger Alphabet

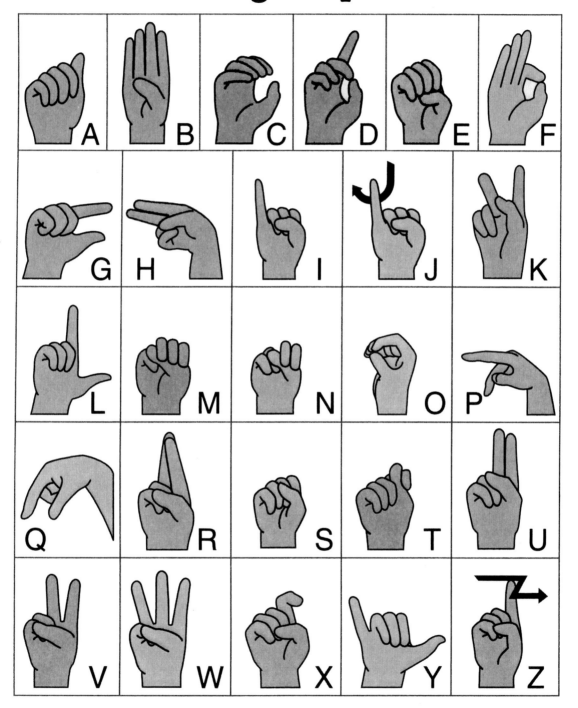

Fruits & Vegetables

Fruits and Vegetables is part of the Beginning Sign Language Series. It is an easy way for anyone to learn the signs for the most common fruits and vegetables.

Design by Kathy Kifer, Jane Phillips, Dahna Solar and Charla Barnard

Published by
Garlic Press
605 Powers St.
Eugene, OR 97402

ISBN 0-931993-88-1
Order No. GP-088

www.garlicpress.com

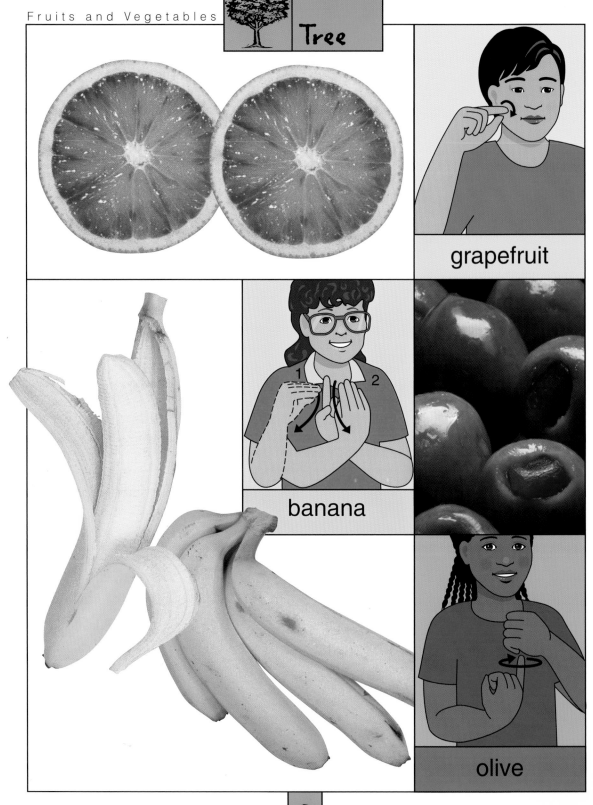

Tree

grapefruit

banana

olive

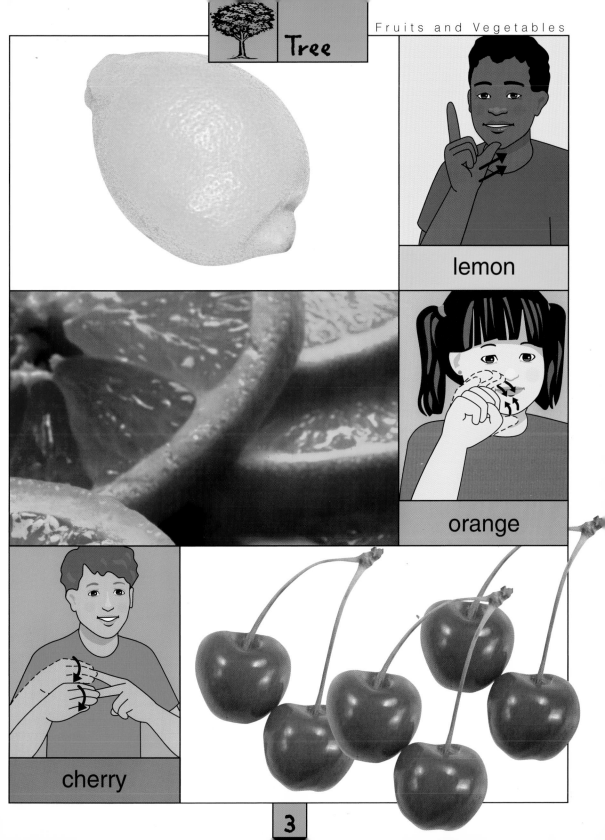

Tree

lemon

orange

cherry

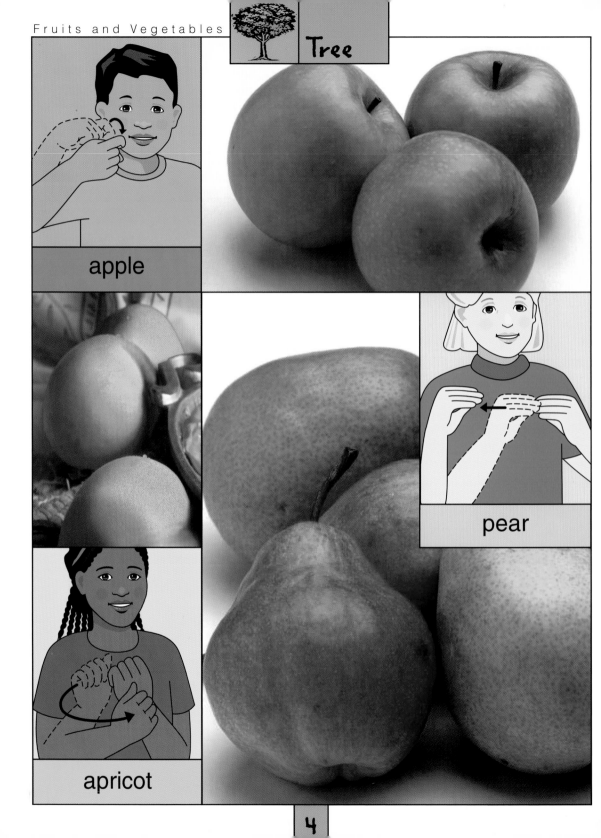

Tree

apple

apricot

pear

4

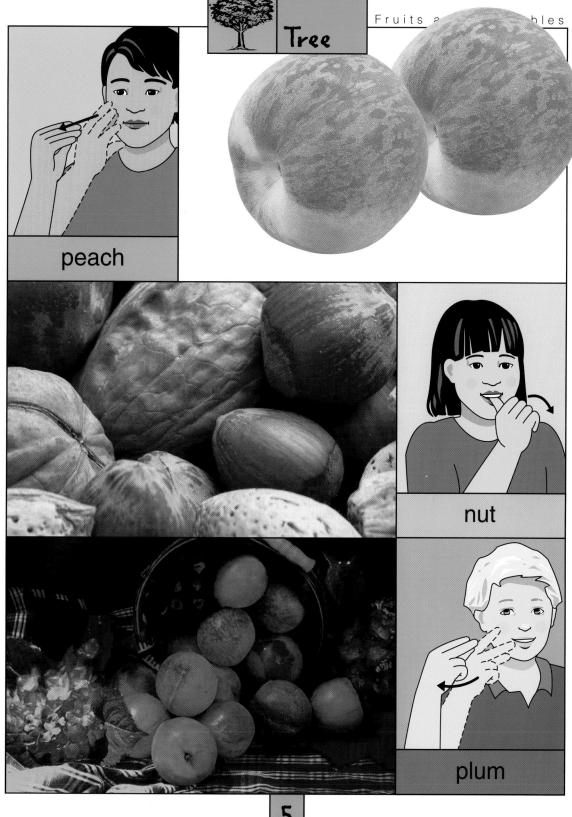

Tree

peach

nut

plum

Vine

grapes

peas

pumpkin

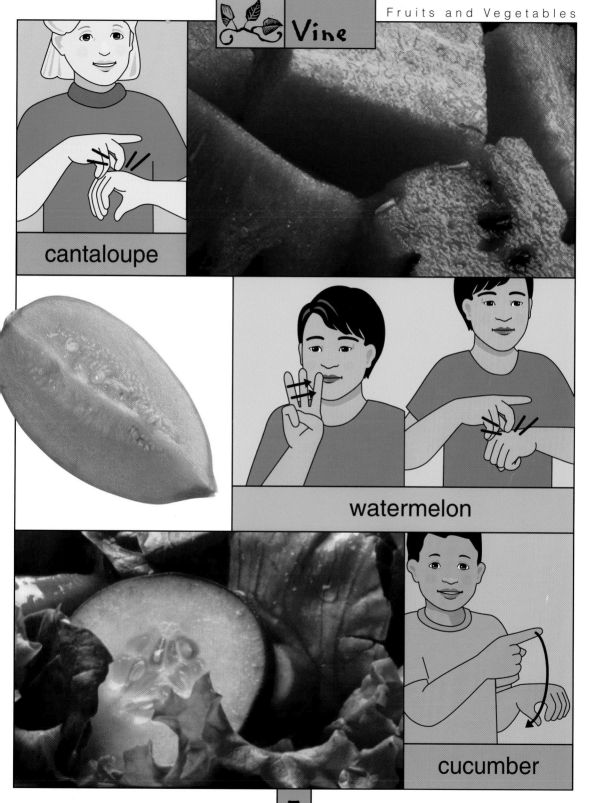

Vine

cantaloupe

watermelon

cucumber

Bush & Stalk

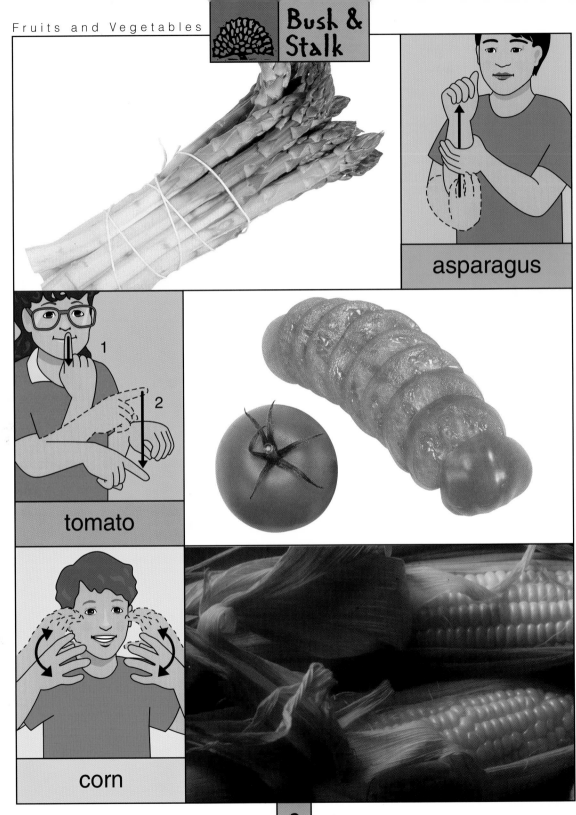

asparagus

tomato

corn

Bush & Stalk

Fruit and Vegetables

raspberry

pineapple

peanut

Bush &
Stalk

beans

cauliflower

broccoli

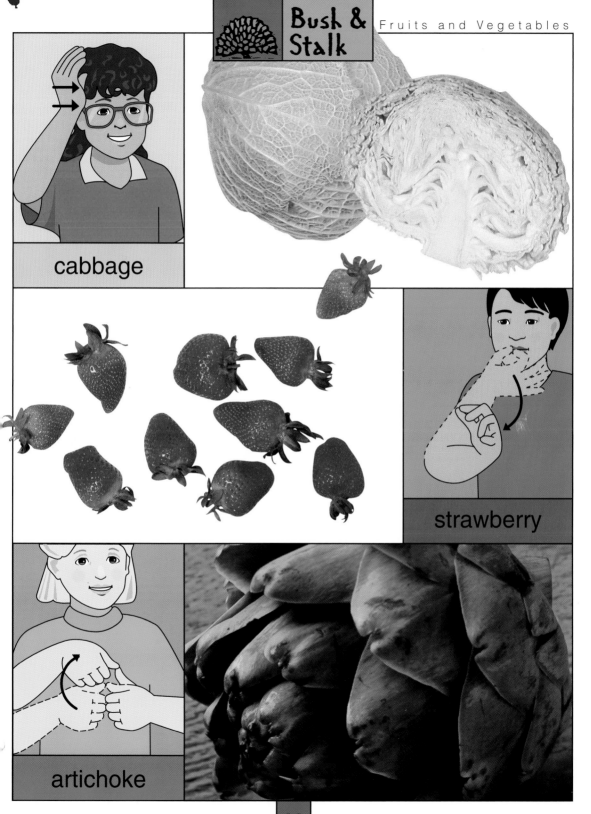

cabbage

strawberry

artichoke

Bush & Stalk

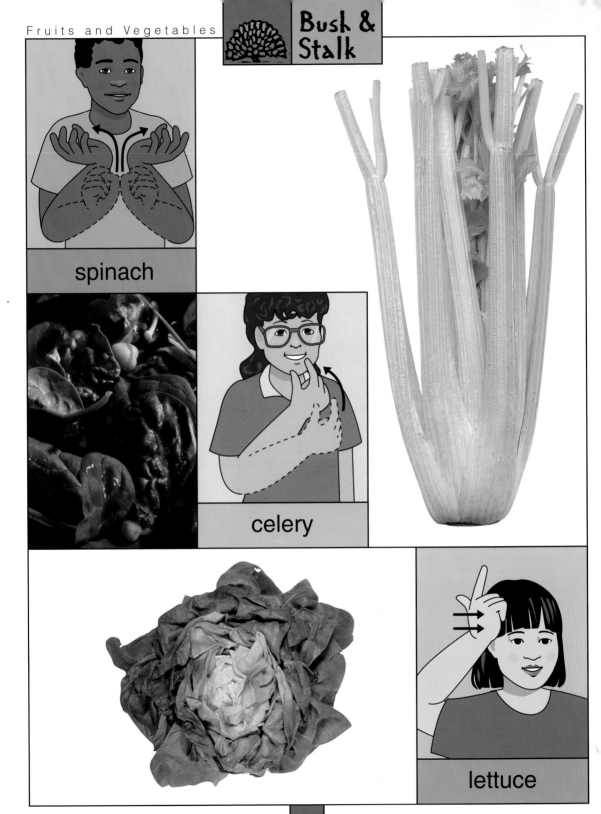

spinach

celery

lettuce

Root

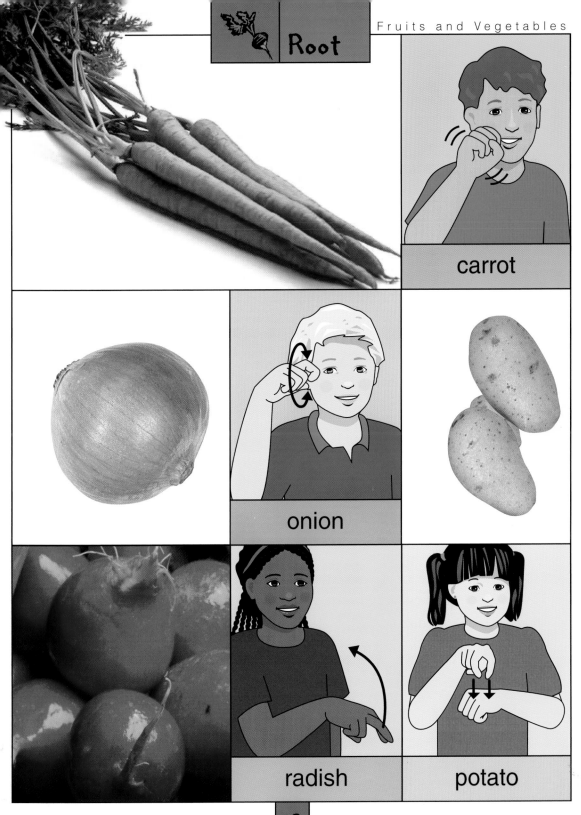

carrot

onion

radish

potato

Other sign language books from Garlic Press

Finger Alphabet GP-046
Uses word games and activities to teach the finger alphabet.

Signing in School GP-047
Presents signs needed in a school setting.

Can I Help? Helping the Hearing Impaired in Emergency Situations GP-057
Signs, sentences and information to help communicate with the hearing impaired.

Caring for Young Children: Signing for Day Care Providers and Sitters GP-058
Signs for feelings, directions, activities and foods, bedtime, discipline and comfort-giving.

An Alphabet of Animal Signs
GP-065 Animal illustrations and associated signs for each letter of the alphabet.

Mother Goose in Sign GP-066
Fully illustrated nursery rhymes.

Number and Letter Games
GP-072 Presents a variety of games involving the finger alphabet and sign numbers.

Songs in Sign GP-071
Six songs in Signed English. The easy-to-follow illustrations enable you to sign along.

Foods GP-087
A colorful collection of photos with signs for 43 common foods.

Fruits & Vegetables GP-088
Thirty-nine beautiful photos with signs.

Coyote & Bobcat GP-081
A Navajo story serving to tell how Coyote and Bobcat got their shapes.

Raven & Water Monster GP-082
This Haida story tells how Raven gained his beautiful black color and how he brought water to the earth.

Fountain of Youth GP-086
This Korean folk tale about neighbors shows the rewards of kindness and the folly of greed.

Ananse the Spider: Why Spiders Stay on the Ceiling
GP-085
A West African folk tale about the boastful spider Ananse and why he now hides in dark corners.

Numbers